Grace in Motion

Cathy Vickers

BookLeaf
Publishing

India | USA | UK

Presentation by *BookLeaf Publishing*

Web: www.bookleafpub.com

E-mail: info@bookleafpub.com

ISBN: 9789358311792

First edition 2023

*This book is dedicated to all of my family.
My parents, Ted and Linda Vickers, for
their wonderful guidance throughout my
life. My wonderful six children, Heather,
Trevor, Wesley, Matthew, Haven and
Hunter. And my two grandchildren, Kyler
and Evren. May you all enjoy a life of peace
and love.*

ACKNOWLEDGEMENT

Thank you to all those who have helped me to create my well needed quiet moments throughout my life. Thank you to our God who helped inspire most of these poems.

PREFACE

Let this book take you to a peaceful place, enjoying nature and all things good. It was written to calm your soul, and relax in the quietness of your heart.

My Father's Hand

We see His hand in everything.
The sun, the rain, the birds that sing.
The flowers that bloom, the wind that blows,
The leaves that fall, the grass that grows.

In the ocean's waves, the trees so tall;
In the vastness of mountains, and the ants so
small.
Each grain of sand, and in the bluest of skies,
Rivers always flowing, the color of our eyes.

His love and beauty shines everywhere,
In this world He created for us to share.
When we see the smile on a stranger's face;
Or feel the warmth of a loving embrace.

God's love is magnificent, and by His hand He
shows
His complete love for us, and His love only
grows.
Just look for the beauty wherever you go;
And in the still silence His sweetness will flow.

Grace

Good works cannot save you, only Jesus can.
Through His blood that He shed, His salvation
plan.
His word tells us in Romans three twenty three
that we are all sinners, and dead in sin are we.

But you can see clearly in John three sixteen
That He loved us so much, He has made us all
clean.
By the blood that He shed, on the old rugged
cross;
His will for all to be saved, and none to be lost.

On that old wretched cross He gave His only
son;
To die in our place, now the victory's been won.
For those who believe, eternal life He will give.
And each day and hereafter, for Him we
"should" live.

So please come to Him now, you only have to
believe;
And by your trust in Him, everlasting life you'll
receive.
So simple His promise, but yet it's so true;

Accept Him as your Savior, and live life all
anew.

Peace

When you see the sun rise, and you hear the
birds sing,
It's another sweet day for joy and beauty to
bring.
No matter what ails you, put a smile on your
face.
And enjoy all your world with beauty and grace.

Take time to smell flowers, and dance in the
rain.
It helps to ease worries and forget all the pain.
The roads that we travel are never easy or light.
But if you enjoy all life's treasures your days
will be bright.

So wake up in the morning, put your coffee pot
on.
Take time to sip slowly, and your blessings think
upon.
Jump start your day with a good verse or two...
So when trials come your way, you will know
what to do.

Just keep your mind set on things that are good.

And with a heart full of love, you'll move as you
should.
Be patient, be loving, be caring, be kind;
And you'll soon see your troubles will be all left
behind.

Beach Serenity

When I hear the waves crashing upon the shore,
I could not ask for anything more;
Than to be relaxing in the warmest sun;
And watching the kids play, having so much fun.

Building sand castles or collecting shells;
It makes my soul happy, and my heart just
swells.
Swimming and jumping over all of the waves;
Peaceful times like these, my heart it craves.

Watching the surfers and the boats as they pass,
Making sweet memories and hoping they last.
When you watch the sun set, or see the sun
rising,
See a crab or a conch shell, everything's so
exciting.

You can be anywhere when you're laying on that
shore.
And wishing this moment would last
forevermore.
Appreciate God's beauty every chance that you
get.
This life's not forever, so never ever forget.

Prayerfully

Praying to God is just talking to our Friend.
He is our Creator, no beginning, no end.
His love for us endless, and His promises true.
His forgiveness is always, for me and for you.

We should pray when we're worried, or happy or
sad.
Pray lots for others, and when we're angry or
mad.
He hears every prayer, His love ever increasing.
As the Bible tells us, we should pray without
ceasing.

When we pray for others, blessings we'll receive.
Cause miracles do happen, if you only believe.
He hears all our thoughts, while in the silence
we pray.
And in the noise and the bustle, He'll never go
away.

So talk to Him any time; He's always listening.
And soon you will find, your eyes will be
glistening.
As He answers your prayers, be sure to thank
Him too.

He's the Son always shining, for me and for you.

8

Dependence

Giving up addictions is a hard thing to do.
But ask God for help and He will see you
through.
Though many our struggles, our doubts and our
fears;
Even those we've held on to for many a years.

He's patient, forgiving, and loving and kind.
He wants so much to help put our troubles
behind.
When we put God first in all we say and we do,
He's a stronghold in trouble, and He will guide
you through.

So don't give up hope, all is not at a loss.
He bore all of our burdens, upon that old cross.
Give Him all of your struggles, and in faith do
believe.
You can lose your addictions, and blessings
you'll receive.

He loves you, died for you, He truly does care.
A testimony you'll be, and with others can share.
Your words of encouragement may help others
along.

And you'll see in your weaknesses He is made strong.

Thoughts

Think on things that are lovely, and honest and
kind.
Keep all of these things inside of your mind.
Soon you will see that your days will be
brighter.
And all of your burdens will seem a bit lighter.

There's no need for fear, or for stresses or worry.
Slow down just a bit, don't be in such a hurry.
Pause and reflect on the joys life can bring.
When you focus on good, it will make your
heart sing.

Do every thing that you do, as unto the Lord.
And blessings upon blessings will be your
reward.
When you struggle with doubts, or heartache or
fear,
Always look to the Lord, for He always is near.

So take a deep breath, and start each day anew;
Keep your eyes on the Lord, He is faithful and
true.
His promises sure, let His Word be your guide.
You are never alone, for He is always beside.

Forgiveness

Forgive me Lord for things I have done, when
I've failed you in any way.
I only want to be closer to You, and become
more like You every day.
Help me to be lots more patient, forgiving and
kind.
Keeping Your word in my heart, and always on
my mind.

Dead in transgressions, and helpless are we.
But Your grace is sufficient, and in You I'm set
free.
You are loving and patient, selfless and sure;
And in You forever, my hope is secure.

You are the rock upon which I should lean;
And only in you, I can forever be clean.
Washed spotless from guilt, from worry and
pain;
Your love and Your mercy, and blessings to gain.

Thank you dear Lord for all Your promises true.
I will strive, with Your help, to become more
like You.
I'll awake in each new day that you give to me,
Living my life for You, and being all I can be.

Noise

When I have a loud child, refusing to be quiet;
And the cat's climbing on me, while I'm trying to
write it.
The dog wants to go out, but it's raining outside;
Lord bring me some peace, let me be washed in
your tide.

So much noise and commotion, so much going
on.
I'm needing reminding that it's You I lean upon.
I need You every moment, of every single day.
Help me to remember, in every thing to pray.

By the time it gets quiet, I don't feel like writing.
Every idea seems boring, nothing seems
exciting.
My brain just goes blank, I can't think of a
rhyme.
Is this writer's block? I don't have that much
time.

So I just go lay down, I fall asleep right away;
And when I wake up, it's another new day.
I sip on my coffee, while the kids are in bed.
I hope that more rhymes will pop into my head.

Helping

No matter the gift, and no matter how small,
The Lord sees our hearts as we answer His call.
He's called us to love, and to help those in need;
To care about others, in word and in deed.

To love without judging, a hard thing to do;
But with God as our judge, He will always guide
you.
You can always discern what is right, what is
wrong;
And lend merrily, and in your heart sing a song.

His love's always perfect, and so we should try,
To forgive and help others, without questioning
why.
With what measure we give, the same it shall be
Given unto us, in the same likeness, you see.

If anyone asks, you should give unto them,
For the Lord says you're actually lending to
Him.
So live each day happy to help others in need;
And God, He will bless every word, every deed.

Memories

Make time to slow down and watch the kids
play;
In a pool, at a park, or at the beach for a day.
Their creative minds need to get outdoors more.
And have fun playing tag, hide-n-seek, or
explore.

Feed the turtles or ducks, or walk around the big
lake.
Take plenty of pictures, for memories' sake.
It's never ending, the treasures they'll find.
Enjoy every moment, 'cause time can never
rewind.

Take a walk down the sidewalk and try to catch
bugs;
Roly Polys or beetles, some snails or some
slugs.
Time just speeds by, and the days go by fast;
So do what you can to make these moments last.

Swing on the swings, or take a long walk in the
rain.
Have fun doing a puzzle or playing a board
game.

These things they'll remember when they are all
grown.
Maybe they'll slow down too, when they have
kids of their own.

Remembering

Remember the days of long ago.
The moments you've shared with the people you
know.
The memories fade as the days go by fast.
These special times we hope forever will last.

Keep these in mind every single day.
Less likely that they will fade away.
Start making new memories any chance that you
can.
Rediscover the fun times, yes that is the plan.

The shades are now drawn, the kids are in bed.
You're remembering all of the things that you
said.
Did you speak good things? Did you speak
light?
Will they sleep soundly throughout the night?

No need to worry, there's no need to fear;
Our God's ever present, He's always near.
He hears every whisper, He hears every prayer.
He knows every struggle we wish to share.

So keep your thoughts happy, keep your
thoughts light;
And you too will sleep soundly throughout the
night.

My Parents

God blessed me with wonderful parents like
you.
You've taught me His ways my entire life
through.
His love you live out every single day of your
life.
There's not a more sweeter husband and wife.

Mom, you're so special, your heart I adore.
You're so loving and giving and everything
more.
Your beauty shines through in all that you do;
Always helping others, with nothing in it for
you.

Dad, you're amazing, so honest and kind.
To everyone you meet, God's always on your
mind.
His word that you share, hidden deep in your
heart;
So to Heaven they'll go when this world they
depart.

The best mom and dad, with your hearts full of
love;

I know you were sent from our God up above.
My parents, I love you, my words can't define;
God made you for me, I'm so glad that you're
mine.

Balcony

The waves ripple softly as they hit the sand.
There's so much peace throughout this land.
The birds are singing as they fly around;
It's a wonderful, beautiful, glorious sound.

Feeling the heat of the mornings' bright sun.
It's a beautiful day to have lots of fun!
I feel the warmth setting in on my skin;
Soon we'll be walking on the beach sand again.

Just breathe in the air, exhale very deep.
I hope that my children got plenty of sleep.
As I start this day, at the beach all anew,
I'm sure the kids will be happy, to wake up here
too.

These are my thoughts, on them I'm here
dwelling.
Oh yes, my glad heart, for sure, it is swelling.
Yes, this is the way to wake up 'tis true.
This is the sunrise..... balcony view.

Roads

Our decisions in life choose the roads that we
take.
The paths are all different with each step that we
make.
Some choices are good, and some just plain bad;
And some create memories for us to be had.

The wide roads are easy, the roads everyone
takes.
Narrow are more difficult, making fewer
mistakes.
If the world says it's easy, you know it's not
good.
So choose very wisely, you know that you
should.

If confused, read the Bible, for in it's defined,
How a christian should walk, amidst our daily
grind.
For it's in the valley that He restoreth your soul;
Put all your trust in Him, as that should be your
goal.

And consider your choices, each one carefully.
Make sure that you venture them all prayerfully.

For if you choose wisely, His blessings you'll
get.
So think and pray on them, His word never
forget.

The Artist

When I look at God's beauty, nothing can define;
His presence I'm feeling, His creation's sublime.
He's an amazing artist, His canvas we see;
Every day of our lives, and how important are
we.

In the vastness of it all, it seems we're so small;
But He's always with us, no matter what may
befall.
It's comforting to know He's our Savior, our
friend.
He has no beginning, and He has also no end.

He's the one we can call on when things don't go
right.
The one you can turn to on a long sleepless
night.
He's our Comforter, our Savior, our friend and
our Master.
Always with us through storms, and with every
disaster.

Be thankful He loves us, as His creations are we,
On a canvas of love; He's waiting quite patiently.

So when you step outside, be sure to admire it
all.
And be amazed how God loves us, when we're
really so small.

The Gift

Jesus died on the cross so that we can be free.
Free from bondage in Hell for all eternity.
This free gift to us we must simply receive.
His blood shed on the cross, we must only
believe.

He paid all the price for us, once and for all;
For our sins which are many, as we stumble and
fall.
Daily we fail Him, but He will never fail you.
His Word and His promises always are true.

His grace is sufficient even if we wax cold.
We are safe in His arms, He will always us hold.
Our sins have been paid for, paid for in full.
Believing He died for you is the only rule.

Tis by grace we are saved, through faith, it's a
gift.
Don't delay, trust Him now, all your burdens to
lift.
He will walk by your side, every day hand in
hand.
Until one sweet day, we'll reach the promised
land.

Outlook

When the dishes are piling and the laundry too,
And you have a whole list of things you should
do;
Just put on some music, uplifting and true.
It will lift up your spirits and make it easier for
you.

Having laundry to do means you have things to
wear.
There's a lot less fortunate, hoping people will
share.
Having dishes to wash means your family's been
fed.
While a nuisance to you, others would be so
glad.

It's all how you see things, as you go 'bout your
day.
You can lift up your spirits in a different way.
Some say half empty and some say half full.
Just be glad you have any, no need for a duel.

Be thankful for all things, the good and the bad.
In all things there may be some lessons to be
had.

Do as much as you can with a joyful, merry
heart.
Never thought this before? It's a great day to
start!

New Song

Lord help me be more patient, kind and
forgiving too;
So when others look at me, they can see only
you.
For Your love shines through in all good things I
see;
Every droplet of rain, every drop in the sea.

My passion in life is to be more like you.
In every word that I say, and in all that I do.
Putting You first with all my steps, every stride;
For I know you'll always be right by my side.

Help me face all life's trials with a smile on my
face;
Always sharing with others, Your love and your
grace.
My help comes from You, who made Heaven
and Earth.
Through Your eyes, dear Lord, help me value
their worth.

In my heart, my dear Lord, you have put a new
song.

All my days, please remind me, to just sing
along.
Only you, Lord, are worthy of all my glory and
praise;
Help me to remember this for all of my days.

Rough Waters

Though I know not what every tomorrow may
hold;
I am promised that I am always ever in your
fold.
You're a shelter for every storm I go though;
Every trial, tribulation, I know I'm safe with you.

When the tempest is wild and the times they are
tough,
I know Your hand's all I need, I know it is
enough;
To guide me safely through every single rough
wind.
I trust You'll keep me safe and secure 'til the end.

When big waves are crashing life's small boat
that I'm in,
Your light's shining bright, still so bright even
then.
You say to cast all my worries and cares upon
you,
So I'll trust you, dear Lord, to guide me gently
through.

You're my ever present help any time that I need.

I only have to just ask, and you'll help me succeed,
To overcome any battle, any doubt, every fear.
Lord I'm so thankful to know that You're always here.

God's Love

God's love is forever, never ending through time.
His love is so great, without reason nor rhyme.
God's love, though we test it, it is ever enduring.
Though sins may beset us, ever always alluring.

His love it is patient, it is kind, it is true.
It's in His blood that He shed, for me and for
you.
He answers our prayers, in so many ways;
When we call out to Him on our difficult days.

In love He can hear our each and every desire.
With love He will answer, and help us to inspire.
We need only to listen, and just to be still.
Read the Bible and all of His truths He'll reveal.

Through all of life's problems, on Him we can
trust.
On only Him to rely, it's a given, a must.
Only His love is pure, only His love's divine;
His love is for always, and it's yours and it's
mine.

9 789358 311792